THE
PARANORMAL

Sarah Fleming

Editorial consultants: Cliff Moon,
Lorraine Petersen and Frances Ridley

RISING★STARS

nasen
NASEN House, 4/5 Amber Business Village, Amber Close, Amington, Tamworth, Staffordshire B77 4RP

Rising Stars UK Ltd.
22 Grafton Street, London W1S 4EX
www.risingstars-uk.com

Published 2007

Cover design: Button plc
Cover images: Alamy
Text design and typesetting: Andy Wilson
Publisher: Gill Budgell
Project management and editorial: Lesley Densham
Editing: Clare Robertson
Editorial consultants: Cliff Moon, Lorraine Petersen and Frances Ridley
Illustrations: Morena Chiacchiera: pages 24–25, 30–31, 34–37
Oxford Illustrators and Designers: pages 19, 20–21
Paul McCaffrey: page 28
Photos: Alamy: pages 9, 13, 22, 26–27, 28, 32, 38, 41
Corbis: 4–5, 6, 10, 13, 14, 16–17, 26, 40, 42
Getty Images: 8, 9, 12
Kobal: 11, 29
TopFoto: 6, 7, 15, 18, 22, 23, 33, 39, 43

British Library Cataloguing in Publication Data.
A CIP record for this book is available from the British Library.

ISBN: 978-1-84680-191-4

Printed by Craft Print International Limited, Singapore

Contents

The paranormal

Ghosts and monsters ... vampires and werewolves ... people with special powers. All these things are **paranormal**.

They cannot be explained by science.

Some people
believe in
the paranormal.

There are many
stories about it.

But there is no
real **proof** that
the paranormal
exists.

Ghosts

Some people believe that they have seen ghosts.

They say that ghosts are the **spirits** of the dead.

People say Anne Boleyn's ghost haunts the Tower of London. She was beheaded here by her husband, Henry VIII.

This photo is supposed to show a ghost called 'The Brown Lady'.

There are many stories and films about ghosts.

Scooby Doo and the kids from Mystery Inc chase ghosts for a living.

The ghosts always turn out to be **hoaxes**.

The ghosts are not hoaxes in Harry Potter's world!

People say they have seen ghosts in all sorts of places.

Some places are famous for being haunted, and tourists visit them hoping they might see a ghost.

These places can make a lot of money from their ghosts!

Alcatraz island, USA, has hundreds of ghosts! It used to be a prison. One story says that a prisoner called out in the night. He said a ghost was in his cell. The next morning he was found dead.

Bangkok airport was built on an old **cemetery**. The builders said they saw ghosts. In 2006, 99 Buddhist monks prayed before the airport opened. They hoped they could calm down the **spirits**.

Mediums

A **medium** is someone who says they can talk to the dead.

People visit mediums because they want to talk to dead friends and loved ones.

Paranormal fact!

Some police forces use mediums to help them to solve crimes.

Many people believe that mediums
are fakes. They think that
the mediums make money out of
other people's grief.

Whoopie Goldberg plays a medium
in the movie 'Ghost'. At first, she is
a fake. Then a dead man really
does contact her. He wants her to
warn his girlfriend that she's in
danger.

Dowsing

Dowsers are people who say they can find things hidden underground.

They find water, oil, metal, **gemstones** and other hidden objects.

Dowsers use different things to help them.

A wooden 'Y-stick'

The end of the stick bends down when there is something under the ground.

The rods cross when there is something under the ground.

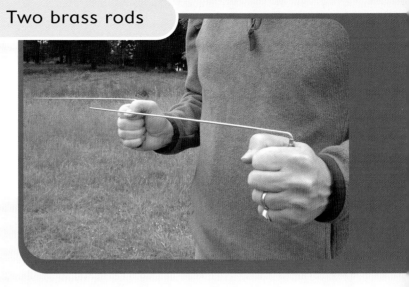

A map and a **pendulum**

The pendulum moves in a different way when it is over the right place on the map.

Many people don't believe
that dowsing works.

Others think it is a useful skill.

The police sometimes ask dowsers
to search for bodies and clues.

Some oil companies hire dowsers to tell them where to drill oil wells.

Some armies train troops to dowse. The US army have trained troops to dowse for water and for **landmines**.

Paranormal fact!

The ancient Egyptians used dowsing rods over 3,000 years ago.

Monsters and cryptids

There are many wild places in the world.

And in every wild place there are stories about a 'monster'.

It is usually huge, hairy and fierce.

And it is usually difficult to find.

There won't be any **proof** that it **exists** — but there will be plenty of stories and reports!

Animals and monsters like this are called **cryptids**.

The word 'cryptid' comes from the Greek word for 'hidden'.

The thylacine

A **cryptid** that might **exist** is the thylacine.

The thylacine was also called
the Tasmanian tiger.

It used to live in Tasmania.
But men hunted it for its fur
and it became **extinct** in 1936.

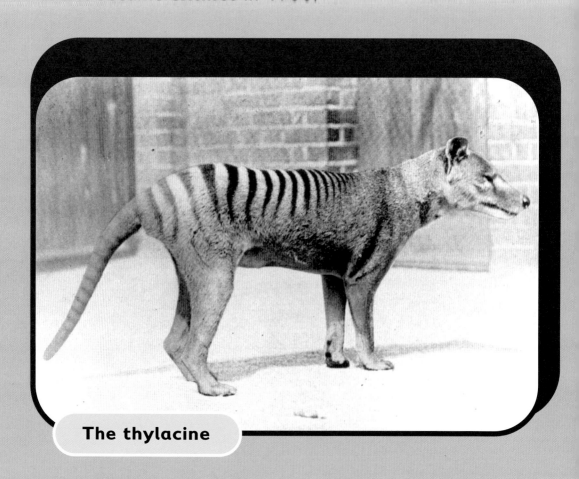

The thylacine

Many people have reported seeing thylacine since 1936. Thylacine have been seen in Tasmania. They have also been seen in western Australia — where they are not supposed to have lived for 2,000 years!

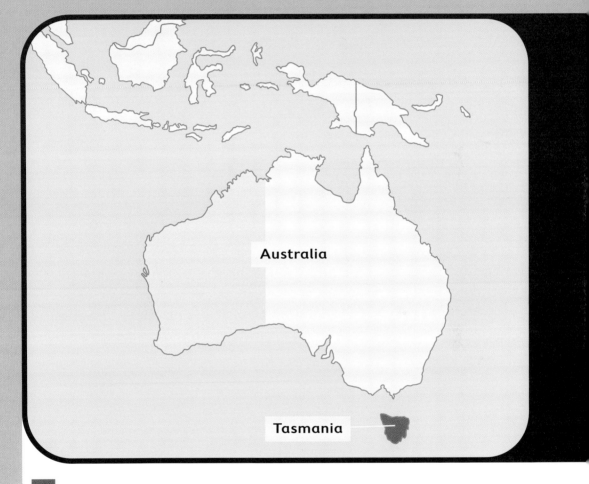

= extinct since 1936 but recent sightings

= not seen here for 2000 years until recent sightings

So maybe the thylacine is not extinct at all.

Ape men

Humans are the only apes that walk on two feet ... we think.

Big Foot

Many people say they have found 'Big Foot' tracks.

Is there a giant ape man in North America?

North America

But large, walking apes have been spotted all over the world.

Do these apes really **exist**?

There are lots of stories but not much **proof**.

The Yeti

There have been stories about the Yeti for centuries. People claim to have seen its footprints in the snow.

The Yeren

The Chinese believe that the Yeren grabs you — and faints! Later, it wakes up and eats you.

China

Himalayas

The Yowie

In 1971, airmen found large, fresh footprints on top of a mountain. No man could have been there. Was it the Yowie?

Australia

Other monsters

There are stories of monsters living in oceans, deserts and lakes.

Sea monsters

People have always told stories of sea monsters.

We have not fully explored the seas.

Maybe we will find **proof** of real monsters under the waves!

Many sea creatures are huge and people could mistake them for monsters.

Death worm

People say a 'death worm' lives under the sand in the Gobi desert. It erupts out of the sand to eat cows, camels — and even people!

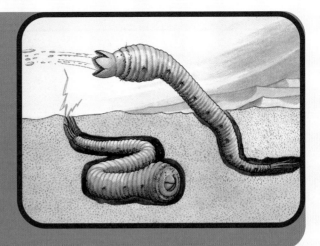

The Loch Ness Monster

Loch Ness is a huge lake in Scotland. Many people have reported seeing a monster in Loch Ness.
The loch is very deep and it's difficult to search in the cold, dark water. There is still no proof that the Loch Ness Monster **exists** — or doesn't exist.

This photo is a fake. The **hoaxes** make it difficult to work out if **Nessie** exists.

Car Keys and Radiators (Part one)

"Where are the car keys?" shouted Dad, yet again.

"Same place as Lucy's doll," I muttered to myself.

We were renting a cottage in Scotland for the holidays. Miles from anywhere. Not my idea.

I really wanted find the car keys. Dad said he'd drive us to a climbing wall. Better than being stuck on a mountain in this cottage. Things kept going missing, and someone kept turning off the radiators. Dad blamed me – but why would I want to be cold?

"Have you asked the fairies for them back?"

We all swung round. Leaning in through the open window was a little old lady. She had a big nose, big blue eyes, and skin as wrinkled as my unmade bed. She wore a black shawl pinned with a big green brooch.

Continued on page 30

Strange people

Vampires

Some **paranormal** creatures look like human beings.

Vampires

Vampires look like humans – but they drink human blood! Vampires hate the sunlight, so they have very pale skins. They have fangs to bite people's necks.

There is a real illness called porphyria. Sufferers have these symptoms:

- ◎ they look pale
- ◎ they hate sunlight
- ◎ their gums get smaller, so their teeth look longer.

Doctors used to give animal blood to these people to make them better.

Could vampire stories have started because of this illness?

Werewolves

Some people are said to turn into wolves when the moon is full.

Some stories say that the seventh son in a family is born a **werewolf**.

The Green Children of Woolpit

In the 12th century, villagers found a boy and a girl. The children didn't speak. They only ate beans. And they were green!

The boy died soon after he was found. The girl survived. She lost her green colour and learnt to talk.

She married a local man. The girl could never say how she and her brother got there.

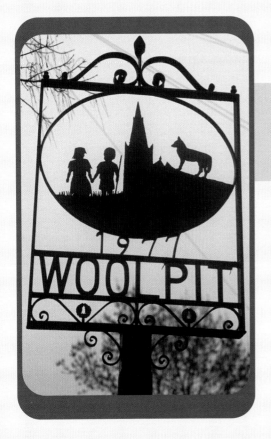

The Green Children can be seen on the village sign in Woolpit, UK.

Car Keys and Radiators (Part two)

"Asked who?" said my dad.

"The fairies," smiled the little old lady. "They are very fond of this house. Look at the fairy ring in the garden."

Lucy was into the idea. She called out, "Can I have my doll back, please?" Then she went up to Dad and tugged at his jacket.

He looked at me. "Silly idea, Matt," he muttered.

"You've got nothing to lose, Dad," I said. The old lady nodded.

"Hmm. Yes, I see. Right." Dad went red and muttered, "Um. Can I have the car keys back?"

The old lady smiled at me. I'm sure she winked.

"You have to say the magic word."

"What?" said my father.

"*Please*, Dad," I said.

"Oh! Yes. *Please*," said Dad.

Continued on page 34

Fairies

People have believed in fairies for hundreds of years.

Changelings

Many people believed that fairies or devils stole children. They believed that the thief swapped the human baby for a fairy child. The fairy child was called a **changeling**.

The Cottingley Fairies

In 1917, two girls took some photos
of 'fairies' at the bottom of their garden.
Many people believed they were real.

One of the
'Cottingley
fairies'

Sixty-six years later, one of the girls said
the photos were a **hoax**. She was an old lady
by this time. The other old lady said that some
photos were fakes. But she said that one was real.

Car Keys and Radiators (Part three)

"The fairies will probably give them back now," said the woman. "When we lived here, we used to keep keys on a hook by the back door."

"Well, thank you, Mrs … er?" said Dad.

"Be careful of those radiators," she said. "Shocking things."

"Oh? They're brand new, actually. Checked last month," said Dad.

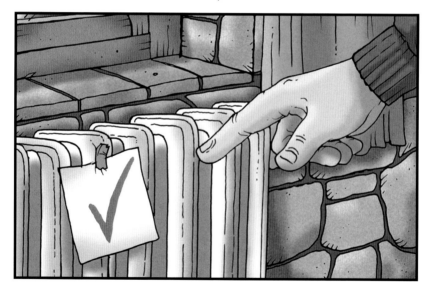

"They'd be fine, but someone keeps turning them off – Matt!" He looked at me.

"New are they? And checked? Well, I'm sure you'll have no more problems with them." Her eyes twinkled at me. "Well, now, I'm away." And she was gone.

Lucy came running up. "My doll!"

Dad turned round. "And blimey, the car keys! On the hook!"

I ran to thank the old lady, but there was no sign of her.

The climbing wall was great. Afterwards we stopped in the village for some milk. The shopkeeper was chatty. Dad told him about the old lady and the keys.

"Did it get too much for her up there?" Dad asked. "Is she in the village now? I'd like to meet her again."

"That cottage has been empty for years. They only did it up for renting last year," the shopkeeper said.

"She had a big nose, blue eyes, *really* wrinkled face," I said.

The shopkeeper turned to me.

"And a shawl round her shoulders," I went on, "with a big – "

"Green brooch," finished the shopkeeper, his face white.

"Yes! Who is she?"

"Couldn't be anyone but Mrs Mackay," he said. "I knew her well. Only thing is – she's been dead over thirty years. Died from an electric shock. A faulty radiator."

Predicting the future

People have always believed that it is possible to **predict** the future.

In ancient Greece, people visited the Oracle. The Oracle had powers to see into the future.

The I Ching is over 3,000 years old. It is the most popular way of telling your **fortune** in Asia.

You predict your future by throwing special Chinese coins. Then you look up your fortune in a book.

Fortune tellers look at the lines on people's palms.

They look for patterns in tea leaves. They use **tarot cards** and crystal balls.

Stars

People have different star signs. Your star sign depends on what date you were born.

Astrologers say they can **predict** the future for different star signs. They do this by looking at the stars and planets.

They write forecasts of the future for each star sign. These forecasts are called **horoscopes**.

Many newspapers and magazines have horoscopes in them.

Dreams

Some people believe that you can predict the future from your dreams.

There are books that help you to **interpret** your dreams.

Abraham Lincoln was the **President** of America in the 19th century. He was shot dead at the theatre in 1865. President Lincoln had a dream predicting his death. He had the dream a week before he was shot.

One million dollars

James Randi is a magician.
He doesn't believe in the **paranormal**.

He has challenged people to prove
that the paranormal **exists**.

He has offered one million dollars ($1,000,000)
to the first person
to do this.

James Randi

You have to agree to do a scientific
test before you can win the prize.

James Randi tests metal bending.

Lots of people have been tested.

So far, no one has won the one
million dollars.

Quiz

1 Who is said to haunt the Tower of London?

2 What is a medium?

3 What would you use a 'Y-stick' for?

4 List three things people say you can find by dowsing.

5 What language does the word 'cryptid' come from?

6 List two things that are different about vampires' faces.

7 What colour were the children found at Woolpit?

8 Who had a dream that he would be killed?

9 Which kind of fortune-telling uses special Chinese coins?

10 What do you have to do to win Randi's million dollars?

Glossary of terms

cemetery	A place where dead people are buried.
changeling	In stories, a fairy child left in place of a human baby.
cryptid	An animal which may or may not exist.
exist	To have life, or be real.
extinct	Not existing anymore.
fortune	Luck, or chance, often predicted in the future.
gemstone	A precious stone used as a jewel.
hoax	A trick.
horoscope	A forecast of the future made by looking at the stars.
interpret	To explain what something means.
landmines	Explosives laid in or on the ground.
medium	A person who says they can talk to spirits of dead people.
Nessie	A nickname for the Loch Ness Monster.
paranormal	Lying outside normal scientific explanation.
pendulum	A weight hung at the end of a rod or string, so that it swings to and fro.
predict	To say or know something will happen in the future.
president	The head of a country that is a republic.
proof	A fact that shows that something is true.
spirit	A ghost or other supernatural being.
tarot cards	Cards with pictures on that are supposed to predict the future.
vampire	In stories, a creature that sucks people's blood.
werewolf	In stories, a person who sometimes changes into a wolf.

More resources

Books

Mysterious Visitors
John Townsend
Published by Raintree Freestyle (ISBN: 1844 43227 0)

Mysterious Monsters
John Townsend
Published by Raintree Freestyle (ISBN: 1844 43225 4)

The Out There? Series by Raintree looks at lots of different paranormal things.

Do Monsters Exist?
Sarah Fleming
Published by Oxford University Press (ISBN: 0 19919862 4)

Websites

http://en.wikipedia.org
This online encyclopedia gives factual information about many things, including ghosts, mediums and many other paranormal things.

http://skepdic.com
This site does not believe in the paranormal. It shows the other side of the argument.

Answers

1 The ghost of Anne Boleyn

2 A person who says they can talk to spirits of dead people

3 Dowsing

4 Choose from: water, gemstones, oil, metal or hidden objects

5 Ancient Greek

6 Long teeth and pale skin

7 Green

8 President Lincoln

9 The I Ching

10 You have to do a scientific test to prove something paranormal

Index